Staring at Fish

CANDICE CIRESI

To the every day angels that fail to see
how valuable they are.

To Kerrick and Tony.

STARING AT FISH

Staring at Fish

Throughout the villages he was simply known as "Light". No one knew his real name. Maybe it was his sunny disposition or maybe it was the way he made other people feel that just left a warm, sunny feeling. Whatever it was, the name fit.

She struggled to find that peace. She hungered for what Light emanated. Light faced battles. She knew it. She saw the horrible things that happened to him, yet he continued unfettered, unphased, unflustered. How? Why was he so content?

Everyone has suffered so much recently. Uprisings in violence, hunger, poverty, crimes, and homelessness caused people to entrench in their positions, fight harder for personal causes, and focus on saving themselves. How could anyone be truly happy?

Days, weeks, months passed. Her frustration grew and festered like a thorn in the soft part of the foot. You sometimes forget it's there but one step forward and the pain wells up. She couldn't decide if it was curiosity or jealousy of Light's ability to just move through life content, regardless of what it threw at him. Maybe, deep down, she hated him.

What did people see in him? What did he see in people? How was he looking at the world that made it so bearable? Clearly, he could see something that she couldn't see.

She decided to go see Light.

When she approached Light, he greeted her warmly. The words flooded out of her mouth. She expressed her overall disgust with the world and everyone in it, including him. Pain flowed out of her mouth in waves of unfiltered rants. She pronounced her hatred for him and his ability to be content in such a dreadful world. How could he possibly not be enraged by all that was happening?

Light listened patiently.

She continued. She hungered to make sense of everything, starving of peace. The emptiness inside tore her up. She begged Light show her what she needed to do to fix the brokenness.

Light said the advice was easy, the work was hard. But, all good things require work. She asked if the work would cause the angst to subside.

He looked at her, really looked at her, and said, *"we will see."*

Light gently grabbed her arm and they walked down a narrow path. He led her to the bank of a little stream a good distance from where they initially met as the sun slowly slid down the sky. She grew uncomfortable as the bank abutted a very dangerous part of the village.

Violence in the area increased to such a level that the inhabitants holed themselves up. They feared going out for the most basic of chores. The violence also inhibited the provision of necessities. No one wanted to go into the area to help other people for fear of putting themselves at risk of harm. The only people that walked freely were people well capable of violence and ready to prove it. There may come a point when they cede the fight, then apathy takes over creating dying souls in living bodies.

Light pulled out some fishing line and put a hook and a small bug on the end of the line. He threw the line in the water.

She muttered that they should make it quick. It's getting late, and they should not be out here at this hour. Light started to pull on the line, revealing a small fish. Light landed the fish on the bank of the stream. He picked it up, handed her the fish, and shared his advice.

"See what's missing. Act." The words *were* easy.

The fish was slippery, slimy, and flopping. She dropped it almost immediately. She stared at the fish gasping and floundering on the ground. Why did he hand her a fish?! What is she supposed to notice about a fish?

Focus. Focus.

Light then turned away and said he would be back later. She was not happy about his leaving but thought, perhaps, this was the real challenge - controlling her fear. She could do that, maybe. He wouldn't have left her here if there was any real danger, would he?

The shadows grew longer until darkness swallowed her up. She squeezed her eyes hard to try to better focus. She could barely see what was in front of her. Complete darkness was only slightly mitigated by the lighted street dangerously close to her. Standing in the shadows, she slunk down behind the bushes on the sloped bank so nothing could see her. She stared at the fish.

The fish slowed in its flopping and shifted from gasps to faint, labored breathing. She stared harder. Light from the street glistened on the heaving scales. The fish was dying. The thought of it dying scared her almost as much as being left on the bank of the dangerous area.

Doing something this crazy was a first for her. Of course, *firsts* are usually different, dangerous, and daunting; it's the thought that it may be the *last* of everything that shifts the experience to the horrifying. Firsts are fun but lasts are life changing.

She reminisced about some beautiful memories from her past. She recalled how, whenever she sat down, her son would plop onto her lap and lean against her chest. She could still smell the delicate, earthy fragrance of his hair and feel his soft breath as she wrapped her arms around him. She remembered how her dad would hold her hand when crossing the street, always believing she was the one protecting him. She thought of the times she laughed so hard with her sister that she feared milk would come out of her nose. And she cherished the memory of her mom singing bedtime songs about faraway places while gently stroking her hair.

All those memories—yet she couldn't pinpoint the day any of those moments ceased. They simply faded out of the routine as silently as they crept in. When did the last of each of these events happen? If only she had known that any of those moments would be the last, she would have breathed deeper, laughed harder, sung along, and held on tighter. Maybe she would have held so tightly that she wouldn't have let go. Maybe she would have fought to keep those "lasts" from being the last or, at the very least, replaced them with new beginnings.

Now, she is gripped by the fear that this is the end—the last of everything.

She had never truly contemplated death beyond the general, philosophical musings that everyone engages in, as if it were something that would never actually happen. Few serious conversations about death occur unless someone is confronted with their lasts...or if they are religious. Religious people always seemed to press the issue about the afterlife.

She had never come to terms with faith or the possibility of an afterlife. Her focus was on herself, the here and now, and apparently, heresy. But now, as the lasts bombard her with enough fear to assert permanence and dominance, she wonders. If there is even the slightest, most remote possibility of a God or an eternity, why wouldn't she invest minimal energy into studying, into learning?

As her fears swirled around, she slowly succumbed to the realization that nothing was actually happening. The horror was all in her head. She forced her focus from fear to what action she should take - but it is hard to exit an emotional roller coaster until the ride comes to a complete stop. The panic subsided.

Oh! Perhaps, she should probably talk to a pastor, priest, rabbi, or someone religious to try to get her head around it. She paused. It seems fluffy to search for truth in the personal opinions of people. If there is nothing, then our minds are merely the product of random chance. How can we trust it? How can we trust the haphazard musings of other minds evolved by random cosmic chance? She might as well ask the fish for his opinion. But if there is a creator, then there must be evidence.

Action! She should do some actual research. She had always resigned herself to the belief that there was nothing after death because it was the easiest path to follow. Trying to divine the Divine would require exploring so many religions. Who is right? With so many religions, where would one even start? But since death is guaranteed, finding out if there is something or someone waiting on the other side really does compel some action, doesn't it? If there is something eternal, that eternity would start with our *birth*, not our death — making the time of life more meaningful.

That's the action! She will delve into the historical, prophetic, and scientific evidence supporting the major religions to see if empirical analyses can validate their foundations. She will study scripture. There are over twenty thousand ancient manuscripts of the Old Testament. Maybe she will start there. If an infrastructure of logic and science is established, then she will be open to the "fluffy" stuff to which so many zealots testify.

She stared deep into the fish's inky eye. As dark as it was outside, she could vaguely see her reflection in the fish's eye as if she is staring into a blackened mirror. Could the fish see her?

The fish's mouth opened and closed as if trying to speak to her, but no words followed. Maybe it was a whisper. Maybe the fish communicated in low tones. She drew closer to see if sound emanated. She heard nothing. The fish continued to serenade her with silence, but the tempo faded. Slower. Slower.

The fish stopped moving; the stillness haunting her. Creepy. Is this what will happen to her when she passes? People gaze as the life leaves her body?

She pondered. What *physically* happens when someone dies? What goes first? Will she lose her smell and taste first? They seem like the least valuable senses. Those are the kind of senses where the loss proves inconvenient but not life-altering. After they go, maybe then she will lose sight, then her hearing. After she can no longer see or hear, it seems that she will stop feeling. Or maybe, when we stop feeling - we stop seeing and listening. Yes. That seems like a logical progression in dying.

Oh! Is there an action here? Does she need to go back to school? She would have done better but the classes were early, the subjects were boring, and the instructors were not sympathetic. But is there ever a right time to stop learning? With all the knowledge in the world, it seems as if she could always stand to learn something new.

That's it! That's the action she needs. She is going back to school! She will better herself with education!

She continued to stare at the fish. Life from the fish's eyes departed, but her reflection in its' dead eyes remained quite stark; darker black on black but still distinct.

It grew eerie. Focusing on death exacerbated the darkness around her and amplified the shouts and screams coming from the village. She had hardly noticed them before. Breaking glass, dogs barking, and an occasional door slam served as backup percussion to the disharmonious crying from the village.

Is that a muted heartbeat? What is that noise? She turned. A barefoot child pattered down the street, wearing a t-shirt too small and a heart too heavy. Clearly trying to escape an angry predator, the child chose to hide in an alley by the brook rather than face the wrath closing in on him. Ducking behind a garbage bin to make himself invisible, the small child heaved and gasped. She couldn't hear his breathing, but she witnessed the rapid rhythm of his throbbing chest, heralding his struggle.

She ducked down deeper behind the bushes; she did not want to be seen. She did not want to be noticed. Whatever was chasing that child might turn on her. She could clearly see the child's face lit up by the streetlamp. She could see the welled-up tears making the child's eyes glassy and white. From her view, they were glistening saucers flashing distress signals.

Aah. Like the child, she is running from her fears. She misses the peace and comfort that a loving parent can provide. Why weren't her mother and father better parents?

Growing up, they were always preoccupied with working, cleaning, cooking, driving—always focused on someone, some mundane tasks, some daily regimen—never her. To be the center of attention, she had to be sick, celebrating, hurting, or struggling. If the big events weren't happening, they focused on the general routine: going to work, making meals, paying bills, cleaning the house, taking care of the yard, buying food. Those are required of all parents. She can't see anything special about the routine.

But what about her? If they were better, if they could have just focused on her - maybe she would have been better. Why couldn't it have been about her? It was never about her! Not with her parents, her friends, her teachers. Maybe if her friends were better, her teachers were better, maybe if everyone in her life was a bit more perfect, then there wouldn't be so much missing in her life. Those flawed people made her flawed.

Hmm. She wondered if other people would claim they are flawed because she isn't perfect. Huh. Well, other people's flaws aren't her problem. Those people should bear the responsibility for bettering themselves.

The child continued to strive for invisibility as the hunter drew near. The angry man's sunken eyes darted around searching for his prey. Clearly hungry and possessing enough life to fight with a vengeance, his eyes burned with an anger that screamed louder than his voice. His fierce shrieks were hard to understand but impossible to ignore. He cast sniper-focused shots at all potential hiding places, swinging a belt the entire time.

The child stopped breathing for fear of giving up his location. From her hiding place, she could make out the child's lip quivering in abject horror. The child's mouth moved but she heard nothing, just like the fish. Tempo-ed silence. The man, oblivious to the muted child, rushed by the hiding place.

Hmm. Maybe that's what Light wanted her to see. She struggles with security. Has she embraced the comfort of monotony as an attempt to instill security in her life? Does the same environment and same connections somehow make her feel safe? Is she ever safe? Can predictability protect against pain? Has she falsely convinced herself that money and a cushy house in an upscale neighborhood would isolate her from pain? She spent her life trying to ensure she never suffers but here she is - struggling. Is it possible to exist without a struggle? She had never met anyone who wasn't fighting a battle. Maybe life is a series of picking the struggles with which we want to contend.

How can she act on this?

Focus. Focus. She needs to try new things! She needs to start a new hobby. She needs to venture outside of her comfort zone.

It's hard to start new things. Mainly, people annoy her. When did everyone become so insensitive, self-centered, and oblivious? It's as if people don't understand what she needs, or maybe no one cares. Why should they care? She doesn't. She gave up caring years ago. She doesn't care what other people think about her. It doesn't matter what other people say.

No point in listening. No point in watching. It doesn't matter if people sing and dance in front of her. It's empty noise in flashy costumes. Each person acts out their own drama, seeking the attention of others. Why care about *their* story if she can't get *her* script straight? People accuse her of caring too much about herself. Well, someone has to! Why should she care about others if they don't care about her?

When did the caring stop? When did she **last** listen to others? When did she stop seeing? When did her heart die? Ugh. Dramatics. She knows she is strutting on the stage, seeking an audience. Who is going to see her? Give her the applause she deserves? Scream for an encore? The fish? Too late for that. Maybe her hormones are out of balance, or she has been eating too much or sleeping too little. She needs to go back to the gym and eat better. Maybe she should start yoga.

Yoga. Now all her thoughts focused on her insecurity. She used to be in great shape, at least she was in okay shape at best. She never expected age to take such a hard toll on her body.

What's missing? Well, her youthful figure for one. It's not that getting older is so bad; it's just that maintaining any semblance of "healthy" is so hard. Why is everything hard? No matter how much money, fame, or beauty she has—it's never enough. There is always a struggle. For a fleeting moment, she wonders if these things don't resolve her angst because they aren't the right pursuits. As quickly as that spark ignited, it died. What else is there?

Her life would be different if she radiated beauty; maybe it could even make up for all the other gaps in her life. How can she ever get back that youthful beauty? Maybe yoga is the answer, or Pilates, or speed-walking? Can you burn calories complaining? She would look phenomenal is that were possible! Agh!

Restoring youth feels elusive. If we can never truly get youth back, to where should we direct that energy? Speaking of youth, where did the kid go? She looked around, realizing she had been so lost in her thoughts that she hadn't noticed his movements. The alley was now empty, the child having slipped away unnoticed.

Hours passed, then another man stumbled and tottered onto the street, oblivious of everything around him. He had clearly tried, unsuccessfully, to numb his pain. He cried out the name of a lost love who seemingly left without giving him the right of closure – the right he clearly deserved.

He mumbled streams of consciousness regaling tales of hearts and heartbreak. His mouth moved but the words made little sense. He babbled more than the brook. He missed the voice of his long-lost love. He missed the touch of someone who loved him unconditionally. He would never find that again - or so he professed. He could never fill the void. His foggy eyes couldn't rest and rolled around his head like marbles. It isn't as if he didn't want to see anything, it was as though he just lost focus.

Focus. Focus.

Ooh. Another gap; lost love. Her husband showed so much attention when they first met. After a few months of marriage, that attention slowly shifted to going to work, making meals, paying bills, cleaning the house, taking care of the yard, buying food - those activities expected of a husband. She saw nothing special there, just routine. But what about her? What about the attention she needs?

Maybe some other person from her past was the better option? There were others before her husband, but the same waning of recognition occurred with all of them. She didn't have great taste in men from the beginning. What did she ever see in them? Although, thinking about it, she doesn't recall hearing them complain. Did they complain? Who knows? She didn't listen. Maybe she should have never committed to anyone. Was that it?

Action. Action. She needs to work on her marriage. Or does she need to end it?

Ugh! How is she to know what action to take? This isn't helping. She keeps identifying lacks and gaps but doesn't know what action to take to fill the voids! She still doesn't know what to do but she does see more that must be done.

She preoccupied herself with her assignment of trying to see all that was missing. She spent the time focused on death, the wrongs committed by others, the love that she should have been shown, and the void growing inside. More aware of her emptiness than ever before, the darkness inside wanted to swallow her up. It was darker on the inside than the outside. Everything that was ever wrong in her life loomed over her and pointed blame and accusations in all directions.

She heard a rustle in the bushes near her. Fear overtook her. She froze. She became as still as the fish on the bank, except for her lip which wouldn't stop trembling and couldn't manifest a scream.

Light emerged. Her color and her breath came back. What a relief!

Light asked what she had learned. She noted there were so many things that she realized she was missing – ability to face her fears, the state of childlike wonder, the love that her spouse should be giving her, grieving what she could have been if she had only had better parents, friends, lovers, or work. Her conclusion: she was filled with being empty.

Light said that was not the assignment.

Indignant, she replied that it was precisely what she was instructed to do. She was supposed to see what she was missing and act. She spent hours looking deep within herself and could clearly see many things missing. She simply struggles with what actions are the right ones.

Light pointed out that the words were *"See what's missing. Act."*

Pointing at the fish on the bank, Light said *"No doubt that fish struggled. You watched it struggle. It missed water. You could have made a difference to the fish by placing it in the water so that it could live. However, if it must die, it could have fed a hungry person. Its death would not have been in vain."*

Light continued, *"Did you see anything else, anyone else missing something? Did you see the child missing protection? Did you see the angry man who has not had food for days? Did you see the heart-broken man seeking comfort longing for reassurance of love or remembrance?*

All these things were material gaps. Something important, something valuable was missing and presented itself to you. These were all missing needs that you could have filled. You could have put the fish back in the water, protected a child, fed the hungry, or been a soft shoulder for a broken heart."

Light continued, *"Look. Look around. See what's missing. Nothing in you. You cannot bridge the gaps within yourself any more than a tree can eat the fruit it produces. Trees produce fruit for the hungry; they produce shade for weary who draw close. The tree does not benefit from its own shade or its own fruit; it blesses others. Searching for the lack within yourself only leads to selfishness, at best, and ungratefulness, at worst.*

*Staring at fish to see your reflection helps no one - not even you. Focusing on **your** lack creates an insatiable void and debases your value.*

But if you must focus on the bad, let it be as a target for you to unleash your good.

Acting *on the lack around you causes you to see what strength and gifts you have within yourself to illuminate, create, and restore. This is where you find your worth – bridging the gaps before you. This is where you see how valuable you are and how valuable you can be. Once you understand this value, the ills of the world present themselves as opportunities not oppression."*

Light stated it was time to go home. He turned toward the sunrise, gently grabbed her arm and led the way.

The Company We Keep

When we speak ill of others, the demons gather 'round.
They call upon their savage brothers to hear the brassy sounds.
The angels turn with covered ears to dull the sharp attack,
And cede their spots to eager wolves who hunger for the snack.

The demons find an ally in the speaker of the taunt,
News spreads quickly among the pack of the newest place to haunt.
They crouch around the rumors and pounce in dark discord.
Knowing to attack another is an offense unto the Lord.

The angels stand on higher ground, unwilling to conspire.
Leaving us in darkness with the company we desire.
The meanness we cast on others comes back to us, its true.
If you look for good, you'll find it. Look for evil, it finds you.

Bad Deal

It's really quite odd, he said they'd be like God
If they ate from the tree in the middle.
It couldn't be great, when did the snake partake
Of the wares he intended to peddle?

They only knew good - as with God we all should -
But they thought there was something much more.
They completed the task, got just what they asked-
The evil they didn't know before.

With everything right and perfect in sight,
They missed all the fortune they had.
But how did they feel about a contracted deal
Where the bill of goods was for bad?

The Game of Life

Life is not a spectator sport to be appraised and appreciated from the comfort of our seats. Watching others compete requires no skill or proficiency. We are not to critique players for their failures or overly praise them for their contribution to a team sport. The opinions of the spectator have little impact on the score.

Similarly, God is not a vendor scanning the stadium to see what worthy attendee is in need of refreshments or amenities. God is not a sedative leading us to a life of comfort and numbness.

Life demands active participation in this team sport. We struggle, we sweat, we succeed, we fail. Pressure is not a sign of a problem. Pressure is the result of getting closer to the goal. The player on the bench experiences the least amount of pressure.

Part of playing hard means we get hurt. Sometimes we get hurt because we are still learning the plays, we aren't paying attention, and sometimes because some random sack hits us out of the blue. Pain isn't evidence of lack of God any more than it is evidence of a lack of a coach. It's evidence of participation.

When the game is over, we do not fall into indulgence. We wipe off the mud, tend to our wounds, and train. We strengthen our weaknesses, we study the competition. Though we may lose games, we grow better with each challenge, both as individuals and as teammates. We learn that the success or failure of any game is not only about our individual contribution but also how we work with and encourage our teammates. We cannot win the game alone but we should never fail to give it our all for the sake of the game and the players depending on us.

God is on our offense, our defense, and the very ball we carry. We take refuge in His ability to protect, defend, and to move the ball down the field - but never to numb.